SECRETS OF THE ANIMAL WORLD

BABY BIRDS
Growing and Flying

by Eulalia García
Illustrated by Gabriel Casadevall and Ali Garousi

Gareth Stevens Publishing
A WORLD ALMANAC EDUCATION GROUP COMPANY

Please visit our web site at: www.garethstevens.com
For a free color catalog describing Gareth Stevens Publishing's
list of high-quality books and multimedia programs,
call 1-800-542-2595 or fax your request to (414) 332-3567.

The editor would like to extend special thanks to Jan W. Rafert, Curator of Primates and Small Mammals, Milwaukee County Zoo, Milwaukee, Wisconsin, for his kind and professional help with the information in this book.

Library of Congress Cataloging-in-Publication Data

García, Eulalia.
    [Polluelo. English]
    Baby birds: growing and flying / by Eulalia García; illustrated by Gabriel Casadevall and Ali Garousi.
        p.   cm. – (Secrets of the animal world)
    Includes bibliographical references and index.
    Summary: Describes how birds mate, how chicks develop inside the eggs, how eggs hatch, and how different baby birds grow and learn to fend for themselves.
    ISBN 0-8368-1640-4 (lib. bdg.)
    1. Birds–Growth–Juvenile literature. 2. Birds–Flight–Juvenile literature. 3. Birds–Infancy–Juvenile literature. [1. Birds–Development. 2. Birds–Infancy.] I. Casadevall, Gabriel, ill. II. Garousi, Ali, ill. III. Title. IV. Series.
    QL698.G2813   1997
    598.13'9–dc21   96-46923

This North American edition first published in 1997 by
Gareth Stevens Publishing
A World Almanac Education Group Company
330 West Olive Street, Suite 100
Milwaukee, Wisconsin 53212 USA

This U.S. edition © 1997 by Gareth Stevens, Inc. Created with original © 1993 Ediciones Este, S.A., Barcelona, Spain. Additional end matter © 1997 by Gareth Stevens, Inc.

Series editor: Patricia Lantier-Sampon
Editorial assistants: Diane Laska, Rita Reitci

Printed in the United States of America

2 3 4 5 6 7 8 9 06 05 04 03 02

CONTENTS

BIRD REPRODUCTION

Mating and incubation

All birds are oviparous. This means that the female of a species lays eggs. Each egg contains an embryo that will eventually become a baby bird, or chick. All eggs look similar inside, but the color, size, and number of eggs in a clutch vary with the species. During mating season, the male of a species chooses its territory and begins attracting a female.

Defenseless altricial chicks are fed by their parents. They cannot leave the nest to search for food.

This chick is only a few hours old but it already has a silky plumage. It is a typical precocial chick.

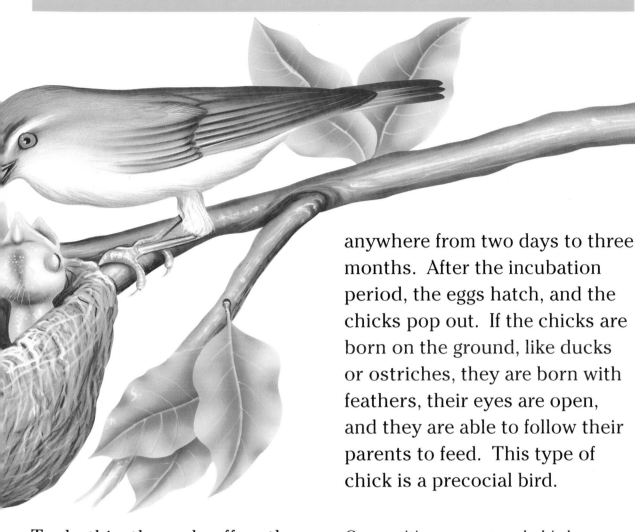

anywhere from two days to three months. After the incubation period, the eggs hatch, and the chicks pop out. If the chicks are born on the ground, like ducks or ostriches, they are born with feathers, their eyes are open, and they are able to follow their parents to feed. This type of chick is a precocial bird.

To do this, the male offers the female gifts, impresses it with pirouettes and dances, fluffs up its feathers, or inflates its bright air bags. These actions are called mating dances. They allow the birds to "get to know" each other. Once mating is complete, the females lay from one to twenty eggs.

The female normally incubates the eggs by sitting on them for

Competition among male birds produces spectacular fights that hardly ever wound the birds. The birds fighting below are golden pheasants.

Types of chicks

Chicks differ from adult birds in size and color of plumage. Pelican and penguin chicks are usually gray or brown, and birds of prey are white. Most chicks have cryptic colors to blend in with their surroundings. The colors of a chick's eyes are generally blue, and its down is thicker than a fully grown bird's.

The chicks that grow feathers most rapidly are the megapodes; they leave the nest right after birth. But the albatross grows its feathers for 9 to 12 months before leaving the nest.

RHEA CHICK
(precocial)

Here you can see two kinds of chicks: altricial and precocial. The rest are variations of these two types. Altricial birds stay close to their parents. Precocial birds are born with plumage.

PELICAN
CHICK
(altricial)

TERN CHICK

GYRFALCON CHICK

SHRIKE CHICK
(altricial)

TAWNY OWL
CHICK

There are many chick varieties: the rhea are born as miniature adults, but even though they can fend for themselves, they remain with their parents for a while. Typical altricial chicks, such as shrikes, are born with their eyes closed and with very little or no plumage. They cannot fend for themselves.

INSIDE THE EGG

YOLK
The chick embryo is fed by the yolk, which contains vitamins, fats, proteins, salts and minerals. Sometimes eggs are laid without a yolk because a shell has formed around a piece of tissue instead of an embryo.

CHALAZA

EMBRYO

AIR CHAMBER
The air chamber stores oxygen, which the chick begins to breathe 48 hours before hatching.

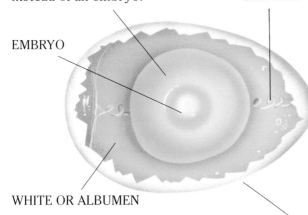

WHITE OR ALBUMEN

THE START OF DEVELOPMENT

AT 8 DAYS

WASTE SAC
This sac collects chick wastes, which cannot be removed from the egg.

SHELL
Although the shell appears smooth, it has numerous pores through which air passes for the chick to breathe. Its thickness depends on each species.

Chicks develop inside an egg and outside of the mother's body. This way, the weight of its young will not prevent the mother from flying. The chick develops inside until there is no space left. When it is time to hatch, the air chamber between the chick and the shell breaks, and the bird breathes with its lungs. Then the shell cracks, and the chick leaves the egg.

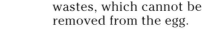

FEATHERS
The chick inside this egg is wet, but within a few hours it will have bright yellow plumage to keep it warm and dry. Although the chick will not fly right away, some can do this only fifteen days after leaving the shell!

AT 20 DAYS

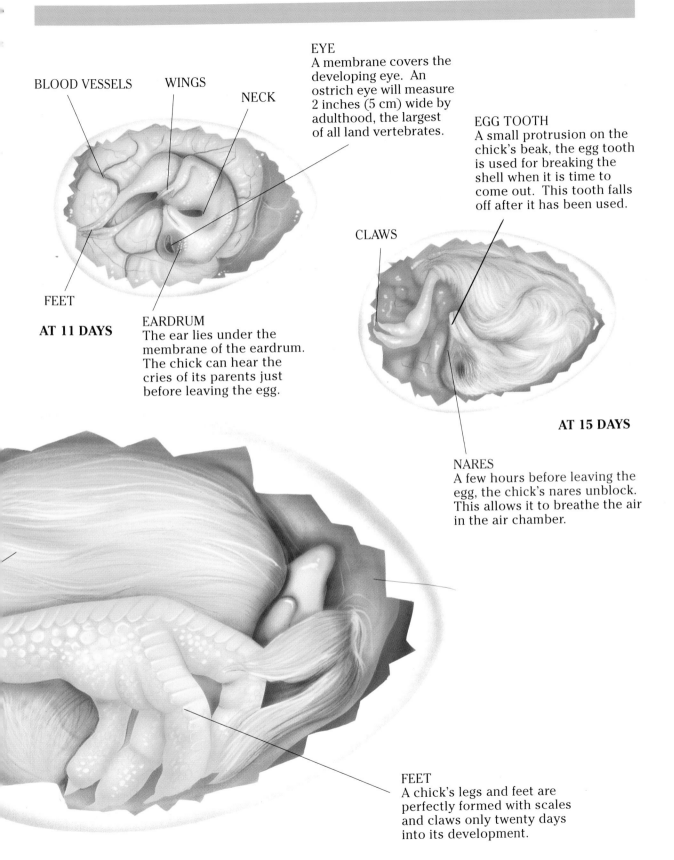

BLOOD VESSELS

WINGS

NECK

EYE
A membrane covers the developing eye. An ostrich eye will measure 2 inches (5 cm) wide by adulthood, the largest of all land vertebrates.

EGG TOOTH
A small protrusion on the chick's beak, the egg tooth is used for breaking the shell when it is time to come out. This tooth falls off after it has been used.

CLAWS

FEET

AT 11 DAYS

EARDRUM
The ear lies under the membrane of the eardrum. The chick can hear the cries of its parents just before leaving the egg.

AT 15 DAYS

NARES
A few hours before leaving the egg, the chick's nares unblock. This allows it to breathe the air in the air chamber.

FEET
A chick's legs and feet are perfectly formed with scales and claws only twenty days into its development.

FROM COURTSHIP TO INCUBATION

Mating

The male selects a nesting area. Then he must make clear to other birds that this particular territory is occupied, usually by singing or by showing off a certain part of its body. The robin, for instance, displays its red breast and fluffs up its feathers. When the nesting site has been selected, it is time to look for a mate.

The male must attract the female's attention. This is why it

The Eurasian robin's red breast, in both female and male, helps the bird defend its territory.

has such eye-catching plumage. In most cases, the females of a species have dull-toned feathers that provide camouflage when they are incubating their eggs.

Male and female partners of some large birds, such as storks,

The albatross, a sea bird, lands only to nest. When mating, the birds greet each other with cries and gestures.

This pair of "balancing" flamingos is mating.

swans, and albatrosses, stay together their entire lives, but this is not common for the vast majority of birds. Albatross couples separate and meet again for the yearly nesting. The albatross celebrates this yearly encounter with its partner by performing mating dances. It extends its long wings, opens its tail in the shape of a fan, and twists its tail among the feathers of its back, screaming and crying loudly the entire time.

that certain chicks are impostors?

Certain birds get other species to incubate their eggs and feed their offspring.

The female cuckoo, for example, lays its eggs in the nest of another bird. The cuckoo egg is usually similar to the eggs already in the nest. The cuckoo egg hatches before the others, and the chick throws the other eggs out of the nest.

The nesting parents do not realize what has really happened. They feed the impostor as their own.

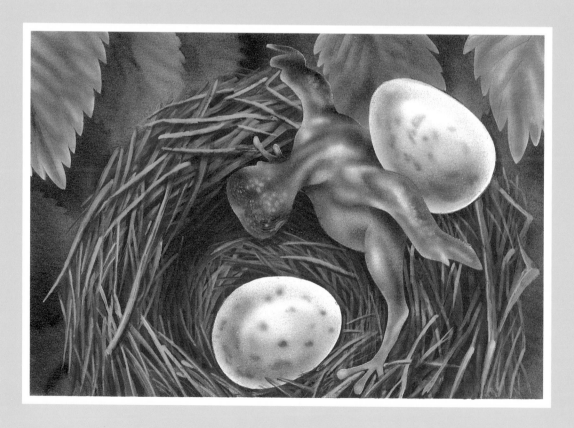

Laying and incubation

Egg-laying can take just a few seconds, as with cuckoos, or up to two hours, as with geese.

Afterward, the birds sit on the eggs to incubate them. Instead of incubating their eggs in the nest, some species of birds carry them around as they travel. Some male penguins even carry the eggs between their feet.

If the parents would leave the eggs alone for one or two hours, the chicks would die. During incubation, besides maintaining the eggs at a constant temperature, the birds turn them over every now and again so the chicks inside do not stick to the shell membranes.

A male penguin incubates a single egg between its feet. When the chick hatches, it remains there, where the male's skin and feathers keep it warm and dry.

This male emu turns the eggs so that the chicks inside do not get stuck to the shell.

THE BIRTH OF A CHICK

Eggs in different shapes, sizes, and colors

Eggs are frequently sand-colored with brown spots to camouflage them in the nest or on the ground. The owl's eggs are round and shiny white, making them easier to find in the dark tree hole where they nest.

The common murre's eggs are round at one end and pointed at the other, and they are laid on cornices and cliffs.

The smallest egg in the world is laid by the Cuban vervian hummingbird. It is no bigger

The eggs of the common murre would roll away and fall off their platforms if they were round. The eggs are "pear-shaped" to prevent this.

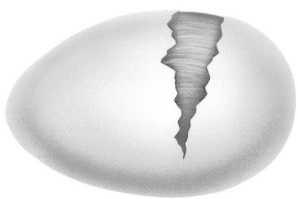

PURPLE HERON'S EGG   CURLEW'S EGG

HORNED OWL'S EGG   GREBE'S EGG

Above: The color of eggs varies. Egg shape also varies among birds. Grebe eggs, for example, are pointed at both ends. The curlew's eggs are shaped like a spinning top.

Below: This chick has used its egg tooth to hatch by itself. Some chicks are lucky — their parents help them break out of the shell.

than a pea, weighing 0.009 ounces (0.25 grams). This is about 6,000 times smaller than the ostrich's egg, which weighs 3.3 pounds (1.5 kilograms) — the same weight as twenty-five hens' eggs.

Some eggs contain chicks that hatch smaller than the rest of the clutch. Sometimes, an egg may have a double yolk, but it never produces chicks.

To leave the egg, the chick pecks at the shell with its egg tooth or turns around until it cracks the egg in half.

that some birds are "art collectors"?

There are eighteen species of Australian birds known as bowerbirds. The males prepare a bower, a place used for mating. The bower can be a plain, cleared space; a bordered avenue; or a roofed-over area. The male decorates the bower with various objects, such as small bones, beetle wings, snail shells, berries, and flowers, all intended to lure females to the male.

The first days of life

Parents can communicate with their chicks days before hatching. If there is any danger, the parent emits a warning sound that the chick responds to by remaining silent.

Parents collect the chicks' droppings and carry them away to keep the nest clean.

Parents may help their chick leave the egg, but most chicks can do it on their own.

Once the egg has broken, the parents take the shell remains away from the nest to keep predators away. They do the same with the chick's droppings. A few chicks can defend themselves when enemies approach. Some, like the royal owl, blow themselves up like balloons, fluffing up their feathers. Others, like the hoopoes, throw droppings into the enemy's face.

This young owl does its best to present a frightening appearance to a predator.

THE BEHAVIOR OF CHICKS

Growth

Altricial chicks hatch in nests hidden among the branches of trees. Precocial birds hatch in nests on the ground. The precocial chicks face great dangers, so they are born with their eyes open and are covered with plumage. When they are just one hour old, they can walk and swim.

Chicks feed on larvae, insects, and any other food their parents can supply them with. Many

The sight of these wide open mouths seems to say, "Here, here!" as the parents feed their young.

adult birds are vegetarians, but young chicks can eat insects, which will help them grow. The great tit chick, an altricial

At three days, these blind, featherless great tit chicks cannot feed themselves. They cry out for food by opening their mouths as wide as they can.

When they are five days old, and still blind, the first fine feathers appear on the head and back. These feathers are known as down.

For the first few days, the swan's chicks remain at their mother's side. The mother feeds the chicks and shows them where to find food for themselves.

chick, has no feathers. Its eyes stay closed up to thirteen days after hatching.

When the chick is three days old, it cries by opening up its beak as wide as possible. At five days, it begins to grow feathers on its head, back, and, wings until its entire body is covered. By the thirteenth day, the young tit's eyes are open, and its body is covered with feathers. A few days later, it can leave the nest and care for itself.

At nine days, the first real feathers appear. They grow and harden, especially on the wings. The young chicks will soon be able to fly.

With their eyes open and their new feathers, these thirteen-day old chicks will soon be able to to move their wings and take their first flight.

that some birds can divert the attention of predators?

Parents feed and defend their young until the chicks are old enough to survive on their own.

Many birds have tricks for drawing predators away from their young. One of them is for the bird to pretend it is wounded. A hungry predator thinks this is easy prey and moves away from the nest.

When the predator is far enough from the nest, the bird suddenly drops its pretense and flies away.

Parental care

Chicks quickly open their mouths when they hear their parents approaching. To feed their young, many parents first swallow the food themselves and then bring it up again as a warm paste. This way of feeding is common among aquatic birds, such as the albatross.

Birds of prey feed their young with small pieces of meat from their victims. The pelican's chicks stick their heads inside the mother's throat, where the adult keeps the food.

In warm regions, certain birds store water in their beak and release it over their young to keep them cool.

Smaller birds, such as the whitethroat, place the food directly into the open mouths of their young.

Young birds of prey eat meat from the moment they are born. Their parents feed them tiny pieces so they do not choke.

The first flight

Chicks know how to fly at birth, but they have to wait for feathers to grow on their wings and their muscles to become stronger. Then they practice with short flights to loosen up. Some chicks flap their wings while sitting on a branch to exercise their muscles. The first flights take place under the watchful eyes of the parents.

The chicks also learn how to find food. When the time approaches for the chicks to become independent, they simply fly away or remain with their parents until spring.

In a short time, these chicks will leave the nest to search for food and be on their own.

The parents take care of their young, but sometimes it is impossible to prevent them from being attacked by predators.

The chick's instinct

Newborn chicks instinctively know who their enemies are. The shadow of a falcon alarms the chick, and it quickly hides until the danger has passed. The shadow of a duck, on the other hand, causes no panic.

The chick's parents provide it with protection and security. If an intruder approaches, the chicks are either defended or taken to a safer place. Certain birds take their chicks away by carrying them in their beak or with their claws, such as the falcon, or between their feet,

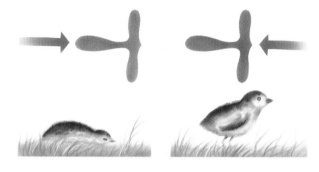

Chicks recognize enemies by their shadows or shapes. In a dangerous situation, the shadows remind them of a bird of prey. The same shape in the opposite direction may pose no threat.

such as the woodcock. Flying birds, such as swans, can carry their young on their back, nestled among the feathers.

Although grebe chicks know how to swim at birth, they are carried on their parents' backs. This way, they are better protected from predators.

APPENDIX TO

SECRETS OF THE ANIMAL WORLD

BABY BIRDS
Growing and Flying

BABY BIRD SECRETS

▼ **Birds that don't incubate.** Megapodes build earth mounds to bury their eggs instead of incubating them. They are watched over by the male. When the chicks hatch, they dig a hole to leave the hill.

▼ **Responsible fathers.** The male ostrich incubates the eggs laid by the several females it has mated with. There may be so many eggs, up to fifty, that it is impossible to incubate all of them.

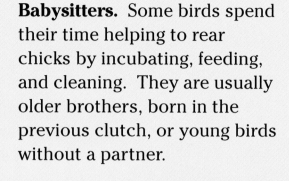

Babysitters. Some birds spend their time helping to rear chicks by incubating, feeding, and cleaning. They are usually older brothers, born in the previous clutch, or young birds without a partner.

▼ **Deadly insecticides.** Insecticides accumulate and affect the shell's development. The female then lays fragile eggs that cannot hold the weight of the chick. When the egg breaks, the chick dies.

How many eggs in a clutch? Some birds lay a specific number of eggs. The plover always lays exactly four; corral birds, on the other hand, re-lay eggs that have been removed.

When there is no water bottle. Birds that live in the desert travel to distant water holes and soak their plumage in the water. When they return to the nest, the young can drink from their feathers.

▶ **Some birds produce "milk."** Only female mammals can produce milk, but pigeons and flamingos secrete "craw milk," which is rich in proteins and fats, to feed their young.

1. A chick breaks the eggshell:
a) with the tooth on top of its beak.
b) with the claws of its feet.
c) with its teeth.

2. Altricial chicks are born:
a) knowing how to swim, fly, and walk.
b) with lungs and open eyes.
c) without plumage and with closed eyes.

3. The bird that grows feathers the fastest is the:
a) sparrow.
b) megapode.
c) albatross.

4. Oviparous means:
a) eating the eggs of birds.
b) that the females lay eggs.
c) the eggs incubate on their own.

5. Nocturnal birds of prey eggs are:
a) brown and shaped like a top.
b) green and round.
c) white and round.

6. The female cuckoo:
a) lays its eggs in other birds' nests and abandons them.
b) lays its eggs in other birds' nests but continues to look after them.
c) takes two hours to lay its eggs.

The answers to BABY BIRD SECRETS questions are on page 32.

GLOSSARY

altricial: reared for a while in a nest.

aquatic: of or relating to water; living or growing in water.

birds of prey: carnivorous hunting birds such as owls, hawks, or falcons.

bower: an attractive dwelling or retreat; a shelter, as in a garden, made with tree boughs or vines twined together.

camouflage: a way of disguising something or someone to make it look like its surroundings. An animal's camouflage helps it blend in with its surrounding habitat, making it harder for predators to see.

chalaza: a spiral band in the white of a bird's egg that extends from the yolk to inside the end of the egg. The egg has a chalaza inside each end.

chick: a young chicken or bird.

clutch (*n*): a group of eggs laid at the same time.

cornice: an overhanging rock.

cryptic: serving to conceal; secret; mysterious; having a hidden meaning.

defenseless: unable to protect oneself.

divert: to turn aside, to distract.

down (*n*): soft, fluffy feathers.

droppings: the unusable solid waste matter that is expelled from an animal's body after it has processed its food.

embryo: an animal in the very earliest stages of growth, usually in an egg or its mother's uterus, after it has been conceived.

fragile: delicate; easily broken or destroyed; lacking strength.

hatch: to break out of an egg.

impostor: one that takes on an identity not his own in order to deceive.

incubate: to keep eggs warm, usually with body heat, so they will hatch.

independent: not controlled by others; able to live on one's own.

inflate: to fill with air or gas and expand.

insecticides: toxic chemicals used to kill insects.

instinct: a pattern of activity or tendency that is inborn.

intruder: someone or something that trespasses or enters without an invitation or prior permission.

larva: the wingless, wormlike form of a newly-hatched insect; in the life cycle of insects, amphibians, fish, and some other organisms, the stage that comes after the egg but before full development.

mammals: warm-blooded animals that have backbones. Female mammals produce milk to feed their young.

mate (*v*): to join together (animals) to produce young; to breed a male and a female.

megapodes: chickenlike birds from Australia, also referred to as mound builders or incubator birds. Megapodes build large mounds of vegetation and dirt in which to lay their eggs. When the chicks hatch, they dig their way out of the mound and immediately start living independently.

membrane: a thin, soft, flexible layer of tissue in an animal or plant body.

nares: the openings of the nose or nasal cavity of a vertebrate.

nocturnal: active during the night.

offspring: the young of a person, animal, or plant.

oviparous: producing eggs that develop and hatch outside of the mother's body.

pirouette: a twirl or whirling body movement.

plumage: the feathers of a bird.

pore: a tiny opening, especially in plant or animal skin.

precocial: leaving the nest soon after hatching.

predators: animals that kill and eat other animals.

prey: animals that are hunted, captured, and killed for food by other animals.

remains: what is left after something has died.

reproduction: the process of mating, creating offspring, and bearing young.

scales: small, thin platelike pieces that overlap to cover fish and reptiles or some portion of an animal's body.

species: animals or plants that are closely related and often similar in behavior and appearance. Members of the same species are capable of breeding together.

territory: a specific region or area of land.

vegetarian: one that does not eat meat; a plant-eater.

vitamins: a group of natural substances present in foodstuffs and needed in very small amounts for nourishing animals.

yolk: the yellow center of an egg that is surrounded by the white.

ACTIVITIES

◆ The cuckoo lays its eggs in the nests of other birds. Visit a museum or look in library books to find out what other birds will lay eggs in the nests of a different species of bird. Why do the parent birds feed the strange nestling? Do all species of intruding birds destroy the parent birds' own young?

◆ Make a paper egg collection. Draw the outline of various types of eggs on a sheet of white paper. Then, using crayons, markers, or watercolors, color the paper eggs with the pattern of the eggs of different birds. Write the name of the bird next to its egg. The library has books showing the many different kinds of patterns on eggs.

◆ Some people collect bird eggs for study or as an educational hobby. In order to keep the eggs after finding them, each one must be emptied of its contents through a process called egg-blowing. Go to the library and do some research on birds and what their eggs look like. This will help you identify any eggs you may find.

MORE BOOKS TO READ

Backyard Birds. Jonathan Pine (HarperCollins)
Bald Eagle Magic for Kids. Charlene Gieck (Gareth Stevens)
Birds. Michael George (Childs World)
Discover Birds. Todd A. Culver (Forest House)
From Egg to Robin. Oliver S. Owen (Abdo and Daughters)
Hawk Magic for Kids. Summer Matteson (Gareth Stevens)
If You Find a Baby Bird. Tara Boice (Seawind Publishing)
Loon Magic for Kids. Tom Klein (Gareth Stevens)
Owls. Markus Kappeler (Gareth Stevens)
Penguins. Annette Barkhausen and Franz Geiser (Gareth Stevens)
Urban Roosts: Where Birds Nest in the City. Barbara Bash (Little, Brown)

VIDEOS

Babies of the Pond. (Grunko Films)
Baby Birds. (Wood Knapp Video)
Bird Homes. (Encyclopædia Britannica Educational Corp.)
Birds. (AIMS Media)
Birds and Their Young. (International Film Bureau)

PLACES TO VISIT

Henry Doorly Zoo
3701 South 10th Street
Omaha, NE 68107

Granby Zoo
347 Bourget Street
Granby, PQ J2G 1E8

Auckland Zoological Park
Motions Road
Western Springs
Auckland 2, New Zealand

Metro Toronto Zoo
Meadowvale Road
West Hill
Toronto, ON M1E 4R5

The Mugga Lane Zoo
RMB 5, Mugga Lane
Red Hill
Canberra, A.C.T.
Australia 2609

Lincoln Park Zoo
2200 North Cannon Drive
Chicago, IL 60614

**Royal Melbourne
   Zoological Gardens**
Elliott Avenue
Parkville, Victoria
Australia 3052

INDEX